BUYING TIME WORKBOOK

Your Guide to

Building Wealth

and Fulfillment

HEIDI MCNULTY

WELCOME

This workbook is designed as a supplement to the book *Buying Time: A Young Person's Guide to Wealth and Fulfillment*, to help you apply the lessons from the book and make progress towards your financial goals.

Building wealth and achieving life fulfillment can seem like an overwhelming task. By breaking it down chapter-by-chapter, this workbook aims to make the process more manageable. Each chapter includes insight exercises tailored to that chapter's main concepts and action items.

As you work through the exercises, remember that this is your own personal journey. Do what feels right for you and your goals. There are no right or wrong answers. The purpose is simply to help you gain clarity, take action, and continue making forward progress.

Approach each exercise with an open and curious mindset. Reflect honestly on your current situation and habits. Set aside judgement as you explore new ways of thinking and behaving when it comes to money, wealth, and life fulfillment.

The exercises are designed to be thought-provoking and encourage self-examination. Please answer them to the best of your ability. Maintain a growth mindset, even when questions surface uncomfortable realizations. This is all part of your path to greater consciousness and intentional living.

When you complete this workbook, you will have a concrete action plan tailored specifically to your unique goals and values. You'll be equipped with new habits and money mindsets that pave the way to the wealth and fulfillment you desire.

Let's get started! Turn the page and dive into the first set of insight exercises.

CHAPTER 1 EXERCISES
BROKE AND BROKEN DOWN...AGAIN

Giving in to instant gratification means suffering in the big picture — and ultimately, more time in the workforce. All the little things you buy today are holding you back if they're not in line with your big-picture goals. This is everything from car payments to daily coffee to drinks with friends. The more you spend today on things you don't need, the more you have to work to earn money to replace that money, keeping you from that forward-moving momentum.

I learned quickly that if I wanted to build a foundation of wealth, I needed to delay gratification and save my money. My early years were very lean years, but it paid off and bought me time later on in life.

As we begin this journey together, here are some (maybe tough!) questions to get you started, so you can see how you evolve from one chapter to the next:

1. Make a "guess" list of all of your expenses. What do you estimate you spend on bills every month? What do you guess you spend on food, entertainment, etc.?

   _____

   _____

   _____

2. Now create a real budget worksheet (sample below).

   a. Go through your bank statement and record every actual expense. Every single thing you see on your bank statement goes on the budget sheet.

   b. Categorize each expense—utilities, household expenses, groceries, entertainment, etc.

Bill	Approx Month Amt	Approx Year Amt	Month _____ Actual	Month _____ Actual
Internet/TV/Phone				
1st Mortgage/Rent				
2nd Mortgage				
Gas Bill				
Power				
City Bill				
Sewer				
Insurance - Auto				
Insurance - Life				
Car Payment				
Gas - Auto				
Car Expenses (Oil Changes/Repairs)				
401K				
Savings				
College Fund				
Cell Phone				
Dry Cleaning				
Food/Groceries				
Eating Out				
Clothing/Shoes				
Birthday Gifts				
Wedding Gifts				
Other Gifts				
Childrens Extra Dance/Soccer				
Lunch Money				
School Tuition				
School Supplies (Books, etc)				

House - Improvements	Approx Month Amt	Approx Year Amt	Month _____ Actual	Month _____ Actual
House - Lawn				
Hair Cuts				
Nails				
Entertainment/ Movies				
Medical Expenses				
Liquor				
Cleaning				
Cash				
Charitable Contributions				
Gym Membership/ Tanning				
Cigarettes				
Weight Management				
Income Taxes				
Christmas				
Vacation Expenses				
Income - #1				
Income - #2				
Income - Other				
Balance after Expenses				

3. Where are you surprised by your expenses?

_____

_____

_____

4. Now look at each line item and ask yourself, "Where can I save money?" For instance, if your cable bill is $120, what if you canceled cable and purchased shows a la carte? Or what if you listened to free podcasts instead? You'd also be bettering yourself and expanding your knowledge base. If you're a sports fan, what if you watched games at a local bar instead? The cost of a beer or soda is cheaper than $120 per month. Remember that every little amount equates to a big number when you look at the big picture. You are committed to the big picture.

_____

_____

_____

5. Based on the commitment to savings you've made above, what can you realistically put into savings each month? What do those monthly savings translate to over 12 months? Every increment adds up fast.

_____

_____

_____

6. Set up a savings account and an automatic transfer of that amount from your main account every month. What other tripwires can you put in place that will help you keep that money out of sight and out of mind? For example, if you choose a small bank that is on the other side of town, it will become inconvenient to access those funds.

_____

_____

_____

_____

_____

_____

7. How can you delay gratification—what are some daily steps you can take to build up your savings?

_____

_____

_____

8. What were the messages you learned about money in your family of origin? How do you feel when you think about money? How does it feel when you talk about money with someone else?

_____

_____

_____

_____

_____

_____

_____

_____

_____

9. What are your money goals? Write your vision for this week, this month, this year, this decade, and so forth.

_____

_____

_____

_____

_____

_____

_____

_____

_____

_____

10. Make a chart with two columns. On the left, write down all of the old ideas about money and success you have and that you want to let go of. Now on the right, write down how you want to feel about money and wealth.

11. Identify one obstacle that could potentially hold you back from achieving your life's goals and dreams, whether it's a feeling or a belief. Try to distill that down to one word (for me it was "fear"). Now write the opposite of that word (the opposite of fear is "faith" or "confidence").

_____

_____

_____

_____

12. Imagine the life of your dreams. What does it look like? When you look at your bank account in this fabulous future, how do you feel? How is it different from how you feel today?

_____

_____

_____

_____

_____

_____

_____

_____

_____

_____

13. Take that "future feeling" and make it your daily goal. You can use the law of attraction by going throughout your life today focused on those feelings, and attracting more of that to you.

_____

_____

_____

14. What is one way you can celebrate your success so far?

_____

_____

_____

CURRENT ASSETS

Cash/Savings/Deposit Accounts/Unrestricted Stocks/Securities	
	$
	$
	$
	$
	$
	$
	$
Retirement Plans/Cash Value of Life Insurance	
	$
	$
	$
	$
	$
	$
	$
Total Cash	$

Personal Assets - Household Items, Jewelry, Etc.	
	$
	$
	$
	$
	$
	$
	$
Total Personal Assets:	$

NOTES RECEIVABLE - MONEY OWED TO YOU

Personal Assets - Household Items, Jewelry, Etc.	
	$
	$
Total Notes Receivable:	$
Total Current Assets:	$

LONG TERM ASSETS

Real Estate - Fair Market Value of Property Held Personally	
	$
	$
	$
	$
	$
	$
	$
	$
	$
	$
	$
	$
	$
	$
	$
Total Real Estate:	$
Automobiles & Equipment - Held Personally	
	$
	$
	$
	$
Total Auto & Equipment:	$
Total Long-Term Assets:	$
TOTAL ASSETS:	$

SHORT TERM LIABILITIES - LOANS DUE IN LESS THAN 1 YEAR

	$
	$
	$
Total Short Term Liabilities:	$

LONG TERM LIABILITIES - LOANS DUE IN MORE THAN 1 YEAR

	$
	$
	$
	$
	$
	$
	$
	$
	$
	$
	$
Total Long Term Liabilities:	$
TOTAL LIABILITIES:	$
NET WORTH:	$

CHAPTER 2 EXERCISES
THE VALUE OF VALUES

Let's determine what your values are about money and life in general. This will help you learn how to align your goals with your values so that you build a solid financial foundation while celebrating your wins and accomplishments along the way, to find the joy in your journey. In addition to the questions below, you might want to do some journaling around how you were raised. What were some of the earliest lessons or teachings you remember learning? What was expected of you? Is there anything you were taught in your childhood that you now reject or want to reframe?

Remember that success and happiness are not values; we often refer to them as values, but they are a *product of* our values and the choices we make.

Values Quiz:

1. Write out your top five values.

_____

_____

_____

_____

_____

2. Write out five things you're most proud of in your life.

_____

_____

_____

_____

_____

_____

_____

_____

3. Write out five things you want to be remembered for after you pass away.

_____

_____

_____

_____

_____

_____

4. Do your current life choices reflect what you want to be remembered for?

_____

_____

_____

5. What changes could you make to enjoy your life journey more (travel, mentoring, volunteering, etc.)?

_____

_____

_____

6. What can you add to your life every day to create more value?

_____

_____

_____

7. What motivates and drives you? Are you reacting to something from your past? How can you turn it into a tool?

_____

_____

_____

_____

_____

8. How do you spend your time? How many hours in the day are you working at a job vs. learning more about your industry or degree?

_____

_____

_____

9. What is the next job you want? Is the work you're doing now moving you closer to landing that job? If not, what are some goals you can set to move in that direction?

_____

_____

_____

_____

_____

_____

10. In looking at your current circumstances, what could be described as an obstacle? How can you transform that into a motivator or tool? How have others overcome this or a similar obstacle?

_____

_____

_____

_____

_____

_____

_____

_____

_____

_____

11. What does your ideal life look like? Write five goals for the next year that are important to you. Now, next to each of those five goals, write out a timeframe to achieve the goal.

_____

_____

_____

_____

_____

_____

_____

_____

_____

_____

_____

_____

12. Under each of the goals above, write out at least three actions you must take today to reach that goal in the next 12 months.

_____

_____

_____

_____

_____

_____

_____

_____

_____

_____

_____

13. Now, look at the three actions from above. Can any of those actions be transformed into a new daily routine?

_____

_____

_____

_____

_____

_____

_____

_____

_____

_____

_____

14. Write out the reasons each of your goals is important to you—give them value. What feelings will arise if you don't achieve your goal? What will be the result if you don't achieve your goals?

_____

_____

_____

_____

_____

_____

_____

_____

_____

_____

_____

_____

15. Write out the feelings you will have when you do achieve your goals. Be specific—where are you? Who is around you? What are you wearing? An important part of manifesting the results you want is to know what that success feels like. When you walk through your day embodying those feelings, you are attracting the results you want.

_____

_____

_____

_____

_____

_____

_____

_____

_____

_____

_____

_____

_____

_____

_____

_____

_____

_____

_____

_____

_____

_____

_____

_____

_____

CHAPTER 3 EXERCISES
THE CHAOS AND THE GRIND

Understand the value of time and make sure your efforts are always the best use of your time. Be the hardest worker in the room. There are only so many hours in a day; sometimes the best use of your time is reflecting on your success, spending time with your family or practicing some form of self care.

Here's a quick quiz to get you thinking about your goals and actions you're taking today to move you towards them.

1. Catalog your typical day. How many hours are dedicated to the following categories:

    b. Making money: _____

    c. Personal growth: _____

    d. Strengthening relationships: _____

    e. Physical health and wellness: _____

2. Organize each of these categories into a wheel. Where do you see the imbalance? Remember that an uneven wheel won't roll—you need balance in every area of your life in order for your days to roll smoothly.

3. Look at the areas that are lacking satisfaction and happiness. Remember that you cannot be satisfied if you're not putting in enough effort.

4. What would your life look like if you evened out these areas? For example, six to eight hours making money, one to two hours on health, etc.

_____

_____

_____

_____

_____

_____

_____

_____

_____

_____

_____

5. Can you still achieve your goals?

_____

_____

6. What can you do to bring more balance?

_____

_____

_____

7. Where is the balance for you between being the hardest and the happiest worker?

_____

_____

_____

_____

CHAPTER 4 EXERCISES
BECOME AN EXPERT

I wish I had learned earlier to live in the present moment and to really value each moment. Also, a lot of people work several jobs in various industries to create more income. In the beginning, income is important, but you have to master something. A job (or two, or three!) are important for skill building, learning, income and relationship development.

1. How is your job in line with your goals?

_____

_____

_____

2. If you work eight hours a day, how many of those hours are of value to your goals?

_____

_____

_____

3. How many hours a day are you working towards becoming an expert in the field of your dreams?

_____

_____

_____

4. How many hours each day are you watching TV when you could be building valuable skills?

_____

_____

_____

5. Map out the company you work for by department. Do you know how the different departments interact?

_____

_____

_____

_____

_____

_____

_____

6. Make a list of the various roles at your place of work. Now strategize: whose job are you going to learn about first?

_____

_____

_____

_____

_____

_____

_____

7. Who could be your mentor?

_____

_____

_____

_____

_____

CHAPTER 5 EXERCISES
HOW MONEY WORKS

One thing I did early in my business-building journey was to educate myself on investments while I was paying off debt. Even though I wasn't in a position to invest anything just yet, I was able to hit the ground running once my debt was taken care of. I took real estate investing courses and day-trading lessons so there was little to no lag time between eliminating our debt and implementing our investment strategies. Just because our debt was paid off, that didn't mean we suddenly changed our spending or saving habits—all the money we had been putting towards debt was now going into savings.

1. Write down everything you know about investing. Where did you learn it?

_____

_____

_____

_____

2. What are you interested in investing in?

    a. Real estate

    a. Stocks

    a. Day trading

    a. Other types of investing

3. Looking at each of these categories, what resources can you use to develop a deeper understanding of each? Where can you take classes or watch tutorials?

_____

_____

_____

_____

_____

_____

4. Who do you know who has successfully invested in each of these areas? Try to find someone who is successful in the industry where you want to succeed and ask them to mentor you. Take them for coffee, and find out if they're willing to share their knowledge and experience with you.

_____

_____

_____

_____

_____

5. Where can you take classes to learn more about what interests you? There are real estate associations in most cities with a very low yearly membership fee that you can join that will give you access to experts in your area. For maybe $100 a year, you can get unlimited amounts of valuable information and advice.

_____

_____

_____

6. Look for social media groups where you can ask experts all your questions to help you get ahead. Some of these are official associations, and some are agents who stay in touch and talk about trends in their communities. These groups are free and can be a great resource! List three experts, you can reach out to. If you can't think of three, what are three action steps you can take to find experts?

_____

_____

_____

_____

CHAPTER 6 EXERCISES
THE PAYOFF

When you're trying something new and you're not yet an expert, always get a second opinion and trust that opinion. Budgeting and sticking to a budget is important, especially with flips. Remember that this house is not for you to live in—it's for someone else. Learn to delegate and pay people to do what they're experts at. As successful and driven as I was during this time, in hindsight, I valued my failure the most—even more than my early successes! Those mistakes were expensive at the time, but they helped me to become even better at achieving my goals, because I knew what not to do. I encourage you to look at mistakes and mis-steps as valuable detours on your journey to success. They are valuable education.

You don't have to be an expert in all fields—in fact, it's likely a waste of your time to learn how to be a mechanic when your goals are to build a party planning empire. You've certainly heard the phrase, "There's no 'I' in team," so do what you're good at and figure out the fastest way to get to the finish line—whether it's hiring someone, bartering for skills, or negotiating a trade of expertise. Beyond just supporting your success, valuing another person's expertise is also lifting their business—you are now cultivating a community of success. There is enough success going around for everyone to have some. You're only competing with yourself on your financial wellness and wealth-building journey, and seeking out others and incorporating their expertise is the fastest way to success.

1. What are your areas of expertise? Make a chart with two columns: on one side, list your strengths, and on the other side, list your challenges.

2. The second column on your list is where you can delegate, trust someone else's expertise, or invest in your business by investing in someone else's skills and success. Where can you create a win/win situation with that person so that you're both moving towards your goals?

_____

_____

_____

_____

_____

_____

3. Look at your budget and your streams of income. What "nice thing" can you afford while still contributing to your savings and growing your business?

_____

_____

_____

4. What are the most stressful pain points in your life? Are you reacting to them, or are you accepting them?

_____

_____

_____

5. Where in your life can you expand your serenity and modify your emotional responses? In reviewing the most stressful areas of your business building, who do you know that you can solicit for help to relieve some of that stress?

_____

_____

_____

_____

6. Always reflect on the pros and cons before and after every investment. By weighing the risks beforehand, you'll have a clearer idea of the types of pitfalls you might encounter. Alternatively after you invest, this review will give you clarity about the lessons you learned. What did you miss? The goal is to increase your awareness around the outcome of the choices you're making so that you are learning and growing from each experience.

_____

_____

_____

_____

_____

_____

_____

CHAPTER 7 EXERCISES
MONEY ON YOUR MIND

Delayed gratification is great, but once you have abundance, you'll generate even more success if you have the values of generosity and finding joy in helping others. Once you have some success, use your money to take people (staff, loved ones) on experiences, encourage others to save their money and stick to their budgets. Find value in helping others to follow the same plan.

1. Where can you find ways to help other people by using your skills, your money, your time or whatever you have to offer? Your specialty is your biggest asset, so use it to help others and lift them up.

    _____

    _____

    _____

2. How are you generous? Are you living in the lens of lack or do you believe there is enough for everyone?

    _____

    _____

    _____

3. How does it feel to be generous and to be a beacon of abundance for others?

    _____

    _____

    _____

4. Make a pie chart of your priorities, incorporating time, money and personal relationships, with an estimate of how much time in the day is dedicated to each. What areas feel like they're lacking in time commitment? How can you change that? To create more time for one category, where can you delegate? Can you hire someone or trade skills to free up your time? As an example, I hired a house cleaner to lift some burden so I could spend more time with my kids. Another great hire for me was a meal service, so that instead of shopping, planning and

cooking, I was spending quality time with my family. If you feel most challenged under the "money" category, how can you change your spending habits so that you can stay on budget and invest so that you have excess money to pay off your debt sooner?

_____

_____

_____

_____

_____

_____

_____

_____

_____

_____

_____

_____

_____

_____

5. Instead of thinking of purchases in terms of, "Can I afford this and still move towards my goals?" think of certain things as priorities. If you are choosing to eat your meals out, then you are prioritizing that over your investments. You'll return to this list over and over and revise it as you feel the thrill of accomplishing goal after goal.

6. Look at your personal relationships. How much time and effort are you contributing to cultivating and building up those bonds? Where can you do better? Remember that the overall goal is balance between working (or earning) time and building valuable relationships.

_____

_____

_____

_____

_____

_____

_____

_____

_____

_____

CHAPTER 8 EXERCISES
VALUES REVISITED AND MASTERING YOUR MINDSET

You know what your values are, but do you know who you want to be? Let's dive in with a little exercise to help you focus on your ideal life and the future beyond your dreams.

Mindset Quiz:

1. What are some decisions you have made that are tied to where you come from?

_____

_____

_____

2. What are your fears? Write down the worst things that could happen.

_____

_____

_____

3. Write out a dream day in the life you want to live. How do you feel?

_____

_____

_____

_____

4. Think of a stressful situation in your life—with money, relationships or work. How did you respond or react? What would the "ideal you" do differently?

_____

_____

_____

5. How do you feel when someone else wins or succeeds? For example, someone you work with gets a promotion or a friend gets a new car from their parents.

    _____

    _____

    _____

6. When was the last time you did something nice for someone without expecting something in return? This should be something other than a birthday or holiday gift.

    _____

    _____

    _____

7. Where are some areas in your life that you can be generous with your time or knowledge? Do you ever volunteer your time serving others?

    _____

    _____

    _____

8. Go through your house or room and pick three to five things that would make someone else happy. Give them away!

    _____

    _____

    _____

9. Think of three things that went "wrong" in the past. Write down how they made you feel at the time. Now write down how the ideal, future you—one who is confident, grateful and believes that there is enough for everyone—would respond to these challenges.

    _____

    _____

    _____

    _____

    _____

10. Write down 10 things that you are grateful for. I recommend starting each and every day with this exercise!

_____

_____

_____

_____

_____

_____

_____

_____

_____

_____

_____

_____

_____

_____

_____

_____

_____

_____

_____

_____

_____

_____

CHAPTER 9 EXERCISES
SOMEDAY IS NOW

Time is not guaranteed. You should spend each and every day loving your life and living in abundance and joy. Here are some exercises to help you start each day on the right foot.

Affirmation Exercises:

1. Write yourself a letter of praise. Identify specific attributes and successes that have helped to shape your life up to now. Write this as though you are 20 years older and so proud of all that you've accomplished. Imagine you are your own parent, and write everything you wish you heard every day from someone who is so proud of you.

_____

_____

_____

_____

_____

_____

_____

_____

_____

_____

_____

_____

_____

_____

_____

_____

_____

_____

_____

2. Make a list of attributes you want to become, and write notes that you can place around your house (or in a journal that you can look at every day) to remind you that you already embody those qualities: *I am loving. I am inspiring. I am generous. I am loved. I am a leader. I am ready! I have everything I need. I have enough.* I am enough. Now you can go about your day with these attributes at the center of all your actions and decisions. What would a generous person do at this coffee store? What would a loving person do for their fellow students? What would an inspiring person do in the breakroom at work?

    _____

    _____

    _____

    _____

    _____

    _____

    _____

3. What is your definition of success? Mine is feeling fulfilled — always feeling like I have more than enough and that I am enough. Maybe for you it's about making the time every day to be of service to others as a reminder that you have enough. Maybe it's happy children who have all that they need. Maybe you feel successful when you have accomplished a full day of work and still have time to take a walk on the beach to see the sunset. Write down your personal definition of success, and revisit it from time to time, knowing that it may evolve over time. That's a good thing! That's a growth mindset.

    _____

    _____

    _____

    _____

    _____

4. What are some areas of abundance in your life? How can you share this abundance with others?

_____

_____

_____

_____

_____

5. Look at your list of goals. Now rewrite them with a mindset of abundance. If your goal was to "pay off college in six months," maybe you can extend that to eight months, and take a portion of that payment and donate it to an animal shelter. Remember you have enough and there is enough!

_____

_____

_____

_____

_____

6. Revisit your list of goals regularly. Categorize them as daily goals, weekly goals, monthly, end of the year and five-year goals.

_____

_____

_____

_____

_____

_____

_____

_____

_____

7. Who in your life is a priority? How do you share your abundance with them? Do they know how grateful you are for them? Practice sharing with the important people in your life that you're grateful for them. Taking that extra step to express your gratitude instead of just listing it out on paper is the most powerful way to build your relationships. It also builds up the people in your life, reinforcing their own affirmations.

_____

_____

_____

_____

_____

_____

_____

_____

_____

www.ingramcontent.com/pod-product-compliance
Lightning Source LLC
Chambersburg PA
CBHW051802200326
41597CB00025B/4652